ANIMAL

by Marcia S. Freeman

ROURKE CLASSROOM RESOURCES
The path to student success

Life is like a story. It has a beginning, a middle, and an end.

Babies are born or eggs **hatch**. That is the beginning of an animal's life story.

All animals eat and grow. Some animals grow slowly and some grow quickly. But all animals grow.

They grow to be **adults**. When they reach adulthood, they **resemble** their parents.

All animals change as they grow.

One day old

One year old

Five years old

6

26 years old

18 years old

Twelve years old

7

Most animals learn as they grow. They
may learn simple things like how to
get food.

They may learn **complicated** things like how to read and write. Or how to use a computer.

Most animals spend their waking time looking for food. That is their life's work.

A few animals have time to play and work.

11

All animals **reproduce**. When they reach adulthood they lay eggs or have babies of their own.

This makes sure that their **species survives**. Animal species that do not live to reproduce become **extinct**.

All animals grow old. Their life story is coming to an end.

Every animal species has a **life span**. A life span is the largest number of years that each kind of animal could live.

Animal Species	Life Span
Arctic Clam	220 Years
Tortoise	150 Years
Humans	115 Years
African Elephant	80 Years
Parrot	80 Years
Alligator	55 Years
Box Turtle	45 Years
House Cat	32 Years
Bald Eagle	22 Years
Dog	20 Years
Frog	10 Years
Blue Bird	5-6 Years
Grasshopper	several months
Mayfly	a few days

Chart of life spans

(Source of information: www.biorap.org and www.conservation.state.mo.us)

Glossary

Definitions

adults	grown-ups
complicated	made of many parts or processes
extinct	no longer existing
hatch	come from an egg
life span	expected years of life
reproduce	produce offsping
resemble	look like
species	a group of related and similar living things
survives	remains alive

Index